Praise f

"The death of my twin sister was a breath-stealing, gut-wrenching, overwhelming loss that I struggled to understand. The grief and reality seemed overwhelming, yet I found strength and comfort through Dawn's gracious words and sensitivity, having lost her own sibling.

Dawn Dailey is uniquely gifted to encourage people who are grieving, hurting or struggling to understand 'why?' Drawing upon her own personal experience, she has blessed us with this insightful, compassionate, and practical guide. When it comes to 'grieving well', she is profoundly wise, providing helpful insights and wisdom. Her descriptions of the thoughts and feelings of those in grief are especially valuable in walking through your own journey through grief and loss."

> - *Cathy Burkholder, Associate Pastor*, Community Presbyterian Church, Danville, California

"Dawn writes from her heart with the realness of someone who has experienced the loss of a loved one. Pretense and cliques are stripped away and the book provides genuine help for those struggling through grief. Dawn's book is helpful not only to individuals but would also work well in group settings."

> - *Jim Kallam, Jr., Senior Pastor*, Church at Charlotte, Charlotte, North Carolina, author of *Risking Church*

"Written from a distinctively Christian perspective, *Losing Logan* offers both a personal and practical perspective on what is at times a disenfranchised loss- especially for older adults. The journal prompts are especially valuable."

- *Larry Dawalt, Spiritual & Grief Care Director,* Hospice & Palliative Care, Charlotte, North Carolina

LOSING LOGAN
Grieving the Death of an Adult Sibling

Written and Photographed by

DAWN DAILEY

ISBN-13: 978-1495944765

ISBN-10: 149594476X

In loving memory of
Logan Wayne Setzer

ACKNOWLEDGEMENTS

I want to thank Jesus, my Lord and Savior, for impressing upon my heart the need to write this book and for compelling me through various obstacles to see it completed. May God receive the glory!

This project would never have been more than an idea in my head without the most valuable guidance provided by Bobbie Pell, whose editing skills, wisdom, advice, and friendship are so appreciated. Thank you!

I also thank my family for their love and support, particularly my children, Elizabeth and Jacob, for their ideas as this project took form.

To my dear readers, I thank you for taking the time to read this book. I have prayed for each and every one of you to know Jesus Christ as your personal Savior and to be transformed by His healing power. I pray God will use this book in your life to heal you and to bring you to a place of peace. Amen.

TABLE OF CONTENTS

INTRODUCTION

OUT OF MY OWN GRIEF

Nothing comes to us too soon but sorrow.

Philip James Bailey[1]

Death and taxes. It is said these are the only certain things in life. They are inevitable. We can't do anything about the IRS and taxes. I know many of us wish we could. Neither can we control death. But when death strikes, as it most certainly will, we can use our experiences to help others with the comfort we have received. That is my intent. If you're reading this, you or someone you know may have lost a sibling. It is my hope and prayer that the God who comforts through His Son, Jesus Christ and through His Spirit, will reach out to you with the love and support I have experienced. I hope my words will speak to your heart, so you will know you are not alone. Know that God walks with you, even when you are unaware of His presence.

Losses come in many shapes and sizes, with varying degrees of intensity. Death, divorce, poor health can result in loss; even losing a job, your home, or a close friendship is painful. Grief, our response to loss, is unique. I write as I have experienced.

This book is born out of my own grief. Sometimes my own grief has been so overwhelming that I've wondered if I'd make it through to the other side. But through it all, I felt God's presence with me, particularly through the people He placed in my life. Several long-time friends were there for me in ways for which I am so thankful. Many co-workers were walking their own grief journey and we walked part of our journeys together. Regardless of the reason you may grieve, my hope is my own grief journey will help you as you travel yours. It's God's way of turning my ashes into beauty for His glory (Isaiah 61:3).

Come. Take my hand. Walk a while with me.

CHAPTER ONE

INITIAL SHOCK

The afternoon knows
what the morning never suspected.
Swedish Proverb

Tuesday. Just another day of the week. Better than Monday but nothing special. My cell phone rang simultaneously as my doorbell rang. I almost didn't answer my phone. I let my kids in the front door from school as I clicked the green button on my phone. A call that would turn my comfortable world upside down.

It was Tuesday, February 17, 2009. Little did I know how significant Tuesdays would become. Life as I knew it had changed forever. It was the day my sister-in-law called to tell me that my 48-year-old brother died. She came home from work to find him on the floor where he had fallen. The coroner was to tell us later that Logan had experienced a massive heart attack before he fell to the floor. No warning signs. Nothing to prepare us for the torment that would engulf our lives. No clues as to the storm that would sweep us up and carry us to a place where we did not want to go. Death is like that. A thief who steals our loved ones away and most often, when we least expect it.

Bad news is always difficult to understand. Wrapping our heads around the very thought that our sibling is gone is something that takes time. We can't believe what we just heard. It can't be real. It can't be happening. No, it's not possible. Please, please, don't let it be true! The nightmare begins. We move as if in a dream. A horrible dream: one from which we desperately want to awaken to find life hasn't changed. But deep down, we know it's not true. The nightmare is real. They are gone.

It is mind numbing, isn't it? To one day experience life with the one you love and the next day for them to be gone. Never to be there again. No more conversations, no more hugs, no funny stories to share, no life to live together anymore. Nothing but an emptiness and an ache that never seems to go away. Death is so unfair. To destroy the life we know in one fell swoop.

Life is so surreal right now. Some days it is so difficult to believe they are gone. We still expect them to come through the door at any time. We still expect our cell phone to ring and to talk for an hour about old times, good times, and times to come. Other days the fog clears a bit, and we know we'll never hear their voice again. We feel the numbness, the emptiness, where their life intertwined with ours. We can't even imagine going forward and feeling "normal" again. Our pain is too great.

The bad news is we will never feel "normal" again. We can't go back to that comfortable place anymore. It doesn't exist. It is gone forever. The good news, relatively speaking, is we will figure out the "new normal." It will take a while, some of us longer than others. But eventually, we will be able to move forward in the land of the living without leaving our brother or sister behind. We will carry them in our hearts wherever we go. But to get to that place takes time and much healing. The pain is so intense. Our hearts are so wounded right now. All we have left is a gaping hole. Our pain will ease up a bit. God will fill that hole if you allow Him. Give Him your heart and let Him fill it with Himself, His very presence. He will then fill your heart with good memories of your brother or sister. Let those memories carry you forward along your journey. Honor your sibling with those memories...memories that have the power to heal you as you walk along your journey of grief.

I pray that as you read this chapter, Jesus will begin to heal your heart with His very self. Ask Him to come and reside in your heart. Ask Him to wrap His loving arms around you and begin to fill you with Himself. I pray good memories you have of your beloved sibling will come to your mind and reside in your heart to comfort you in the days and weeks ahead.

JOURNAL

EXPLORING THE DAZE

Describe your initial thoughts and feelings as you realized your sibling had passed away. Did you feel a sense of shock? Disbelief?

If they had been terminally ill or had suffered for a time, did you feel a sense of relief that they were no longer in pain?

What other thoughts and feelings did you have (or are you having) in those first few days or weeks?

What qualities and characteristics do you miss most about your brother or sister?

What good memories do you have of them that bring you comfort?

CHAPTER TWO

THE WALKING WOUNDED

They who go
Feel not the pain of parting; it is they
Who stay behind that suffer.

Henry Wadsworth Longfellow[2]

Have you been told to "get over it" and move on? Not everyone understands that grief isn't simple. It isn't something that you work through in a few short days or weeks and then you're back to "normal" again. I have been surprised and deeply disappointed in the reaction of others who think you just get over your grief, once and for all, and then you're done. I wish it were that easy. Grief is the realization that your loved one is no longer here. Everyday occurrences remind us of that fact. We cannot escape it. Some days, we are indeed stronger and can resist the temptation to wallow in our grief. On other days, our grief spills out and runs all over us.

Gradually, over time, we can get to a better place. But it does take time. Healing is a messy process. Be patient with yourself and with others.

Forgive those who are well-meaning, but insensitive. The receiving line during a visitation or after a funeral or memorial service can be an awkward time. Sometimes folks just don't know what to say. My brother Logan was a paramedic for almost 30 years. I believe the entire county of paramedics came to both the visitation and the memorial service. It was really good to see them and meet many of them. However, not everyone knew what to say to me. Like the remark about how "God must have needed another paramedic in heaven." I'm sure the one who said that to me was uncomfortable in the funeral situation, but sometimes humor, however well-intended, can go awry. Perhaps he didn't realize that in heaven, according to the Bible in Revelation 21:4, there will be no pain or illness so there will be no need for a paramedic! Let insensitive remarks roll off your back as best as you can. People are not comfortable at a funeral and don't know what to say. They haven't walked in your shoes. Some day they will. Until then, forgive and let go.

On the other hand, I was truly amazed and grateful for all the people that came to the visitation time and the memorial service. Many of Logan's co-workers obviously enjoyed working with him over the years. So many, as they introduced themselves to me, told me Logan was their captain. After quite a few made this same remark, I asked one of them how Logan could have been captain to so many paramedics. They responded that the captains rotated around the teams; he was a great captain and everyone loved to work with him. He was not only fun during the off-hours, but he could keep a cool head in a crisis. I was so thankful to hear those affirming words, giving me a glimpse into another part of his life. I felt proud that he was my brother. So, if you're on the other side of a funeral receiving line and don't know what to say to the bereaved, call to mind what you liked and will remember about the deceased and let their family know.

Words have the power to heal and the power to hurt. And not all insensitive remarks are confined to the funeral. Many times they come later. And it's difficult, especially when the insensitive one is a family member grieving the same loss. Even your own family may not understand the depth of your pain and the ways you are working through it simply because their way of processing grief is different from yours. The best choice we can make is to forgive, knowing that hurtful and insensitive words are sometimes spoken out of a lack of understanding, not because they don't care. Give them extra grace. And don't forget to give yourself lots of grace, too.

In the meantime, we are the walking wounded, going on with life the best we can. I believe the one we lost would like for us to move forward with our lives and not be stuck in our grief. We don't always believe that, do we? Perhaps we feel like it is dishonoring to our sibling if we move forward. By pushing through our grief, we may feel we're ignoring our love for them. But I think pushing through our grief – moving forward - is what they'd want us to do and still carry their memories with us in our hearts.

Sometimes those memories seep into our dreams. Not long after Logan passed away, his daughters would dream about him. It was comforting to talk to their dad in those dreams. I, on the other hand, didn't dream about him until much later. In those dreams, Logan seemed so alive to me. Even as I was dreaming, I knew he was in heaven. It's okay to want to dream about them as if they are still alive and, when you do, not want the dream to end. It's all part of the healing process.

What do you do if you catch yourself talking to the deceased? Hopefully, it's only now and then. Standing at their grave is an obvious place to "talk." But what about other times and places? There were occasions when I wondered what Logan would have thought about this or that in my life. I could hear him in my head telling me what might have been his thoughts. Did I really think he was talking to me? No, of course not. When we talk to our deceased loved one, we are looking at our world through their eyes. Such intimate knowledge of them helps us in our perspective on life as we move forward without them.

And move forward we must. It is possible and absolutely necessary. And you are not alone. I have been surprised at so many people who function well but are carrying their own hidden scars. Until my brother passed away, I had no idea that several people I knew had also lost siblings. They were able to move forward. Yet I could see the pain in their eyes as they told me their stories. Their wound had left a scar that was sensitive to touch, yet they were on the road to healing and their walk with grief comforted me. I knew they understood the pain I was feeling. Their own journey from the dark and lonely side of grief gave me hope that, one day too, I would find that "new normal" and be able to carry the scars forward while leaving the gaping wound behind. God understands our pain. His heart hurts when our heart hurts. Lamentations 3:22-23 tells us "his compassions never fail. They are new every morning." Experience God's presence, compassion, and faithfulness for yourself. Every day.

JOURNAL

EXPLORING THE HEALING

Read Lamentations 3:19-23. "I remember my affliction and my wandering, the bitterness and the gall. I well remember them, and my soul is downcast within me. Yet this I call to mind and therefore I have hope: Because of the Lord's great love we are not consumed, for his compassions never fail. They are new every morning; great is your faithfulness."

Life as you know it has changed. What is it like on a day-to-day basis now?

What do you remember of the funeral or memorial service? What impressions or images stand out for you? What positive comments do you recall about your loved one?

Do you feel God's loving presence with you? If not, write a prayer asking God to wrap His loving arms around you and walk with you today. Reflect on that prayer throughout the day. He is willing and able to love you just where you are.

Who do you need to forgive for careless and insensitive remarks?

What step or steps do you need to take today to start your healing process?

CHAPTER THREE

QUESTIONING GOD

*The Lord is good, therefore all that He does must be good,
no matter how it looks,
and I can wait for His explanations.*

Hannah Whitall Smith[3]

God is a God of comfort. He can and will comfort us if we let Him. That's all well and good, you say. If He is God, then why did He let my loved one die? This is probably the most difficult of all questions to answer. Certainly there is no easy answer. And sometimes there is no answer at all.

I won't pretend to know the answers. I've asked myself questions like these many times over the years. Why did my high school friend die at the hands of her boyfriend?

Why did a drunk driver hit a co-worker who was 8 months pregnant with her first child, killing both mother and child? Why did two of my friends have babies that died in utero? Why did my uncle die in a war at the age of 21? Why did my brother die from a massive heart attack at the age of 48? If God is all-powerful, why didn't He stop all these things from happening? We all have questions like these.

It is okay to ask God questions. He cares about our concerns. Question God all you need to...He can handle it. You may find the answer you need. You will probably feel better for at least having articulated your thoughts.

We live in a fallen world. It is definitely not the Garden of Eden anymore. From the moment sin entered the picture, we have dealt with death. Adam and Eve did not know death until they sinned and ate the fruit from the tree of the knowledge of good and evil. From that point forward, death arrived on the scene and has been present with us ever since.

Why do people die? Or perhaps the real question is why doesn't God prevent it from happening? I don't have an answer to offer you. I wish I did. I do know that death comes from a variety of causes: illness, accidents, bad choices (often by others). The list goes on. Could God prevent death from happening? I do believe He is all-powerful and can stop bad things from happening. But does He? I do believe sometimes He does. Near misses tell me that He does watch out for me. But still, bad things do happen. I don't think we'll clearly have the answers we want until we're in heaven, and God explains it to us. But what I do know is that God is good. He loves me and has the very best in mind for me. God also loves my brother and has His best in mind for him, too.

Even if I don't understand why God chooses not to intervene, I do believe that God knows our futures. He is not bound by time. He knew way before Logan was born on March 22, 1960, that he would die on February 17, 2009. God, without the use of magic or fortune-telling, knows our past, present, and future. To paraphrase C.S. Lewis, we're on a line in space, moving forward, not knowing what's ahead. God is the space surrounding that line. He's behind, beside, in front of, and totally encompassing that line. He knows the future because He is already there. God is good. We can trust God with our future even though we may be unsure of what that future looks like right now. 1 Peter 5:7 says, "Cast all your anxiety on him because he cares for you."

Jesus knows what it is like to suffer and experience sorrow. He knows what it's like to lose someone He loved. Lazarus was His friend. Jesus wept at the sight of Lazarus' tomb. Because Jesus understands sorrow, He can walk beside us, sometimes carrying us when we can't walk ourselves, lacking strength because we've spent it in tears. In my life, Jesus came to me through three close friends who came along beside me, who were there for me when I needed their strength to see me through my grief. I am constantly amazed and so thankful for these three friendships. We grew up together and went to college together. We were in each other's weddings. We were there when babies were born and marriages fell apart. It takes time and effort to maintain close friendships over the years. We've gotten together as frequently as our busy schedules allow, sometimes just for the day and sometimes for a girls' weekend. I am so very blessed to have these three godly women in my life. They were the Jesus that walked with me in my sorrow after Logan's passing.

The best answer I can share with you is believe God loves you and it breaks his heart to see you in such pain. None of us are exempt from suffering and pain. Jesus said in John 16:33 that we *will* have trouble in this world. Not if. *Will.* Life is not fair. No one said it would be. We will have suffering for it is a part of life. Even those of us who are followers of Christ will suffer. We cannot escape it. But take heart. Don't be discouraged. Jesus has overcome it all and He promises to comfort us. He promises to heal us. Cling to Him for, as the Psalmist says in 63:8, He will uphold you.

JOURNAL

EXPLORING GOD'S GOODNESS

Has the death of your sibling moved you closer to or further away from God? In what way? Why?

What questions fill your heart?

Do you believe deep down that God is good? If not, why not?

Often when we take the time to look back over our life, we realize how much God has woven the events of our lives into the fabric our life is today. It can be encouraging to see how God has been faithful to us in the past so we know we can rely on His faithfulness in the future. How have you seen God at work in your past? How does this encourage you today?

As God says in Jeremiah 29:11-13, "For I know the plans I have for you," declares the Lord, "plans to prosper you and not to harm you, plans to give you hope and a future. Then you will call on me and come and pray to me, and I will listen to you. You will seek me and find me when you seek me with all your heart."

Do you believe God has a plan for your future, a plan for good for you?

CHAPTER FOUR

THE PRACTICAL MATTERS

*He saw nothing but death or the advance toward death
in everything...
Life had to be got through somehow...*

Leo Tolstoy[4]

Funeral planning. Decisions to be made around burial or cremation. Greeting those who attend the funeral and just getting through the funeral yourself. Those are the "big" items that you expect to do. But what about those other details you hadn't thought about until they jump out at you? For example, what do you do with all their stuff? Particularly for those who pass away suddenly, they left things undone, not put away, left out to remind us over and over again that they are gone. What do you do?

When one of my family members died suddenly, her spouse couldn't bear to see her clothes and cosmetics out just as she left them. He didn't want to be reminded every time he walked into their bedroom that she was gone. So three weeks after her death, with the help of another family member, I started cleaning out her dressing table and multiple closets. It not only took a lot of time and energy, but it was very emotional…like we were invading her personal space somehow. But when we were done, her spouse was very appreciative. If you need help in sifting through your loved one's personal belongings, reach out to other family members and friends to assist you. If necessary, pack up the obvious and leave the rest for later. It is on your own timetable.

If your sibling wished to be cremated, how do you carry out their wishes? What happens to those ashes? My brother, his wife, and two daughters vacationed in Hawaii several years before he died. As they traveled the coast of Maui, Logan remarked that when he died, he wanted to be cremated and his ashes strewn over Maui. A rather random remark at the time but so incredibly foreshadowing. When he died, his wife and daughters recalled his off-handed comment. So his body was cremated. The tricky part was traveling back to Maui. They enlisted my help to organize their trip and a year or so after his death, the four of us flew to Maui. We found a beautiful spot along the coast where they knew he had seen and loved….and we solemnly sifted his ashes into the calm but flowing stream that would take his remains to the sea. Difficult to do, yes, but necessary to bring closure.

Five months after that trip, my father's declining health took a turn for the worse. While he was ill, he expressed his wish to be buried with his family in their church's cemetery. I promised him I would see that it happened. He was no longer a church member there, so I wasn't sure I could even pull that off. Thankfully, there was an empty grave next to his brother, down the row and over from his parents, and the church was willing to sell us the plot. So I was able to keep my promise to my dad and one of his very last wishes was granted.

But what would have happened if the cemetery in which my father wished to be buried was full? Or the church, because he was no longer a member, chose not to sell us a plot? I'm sure I would have felt guilty for not being able to do as my father wished. But I would have tried to make it work and when it didn't, I would have had to let go and know that my dad would have understood.

What about those other details: paying their bills, canceling their subscriptions, stopping their mail? There's a myriad of tasks that have to be done. Some, thankfully, don't have to be done immediately. I just now canceled my dad's magazine subscription after he passed away over a year and a half ago. I think one of the most difficult things to do, though, was deleting their names out of my phone's contact list. Erasing both my brother's and my dad's name from my phone was like I was deleting them. Something so simple yet painful to do. I wasn't deleting them from my life. Their memories will always live on in my heart.

If you're struggling with the aftermath of your sibling's passing, do what you can. Do the very best you can and let go of the rest. They will understand. And don't be afraid to ask friends and family for help. Maybe you need a meal or a babysitter so you can get rest from busy parenting. Or help in cleaning out their belongings. Above all else, if you find yourself totally overwhelmed, do seek professional help. Your minister or medical professional can get you in touch
with the help you need. It's alright. It's all part of the

healing process.

The Bible tells us in Matthew 10: 29-31, "Are not two sparrows sold for a penny? Yet not one of them will fall to the ground outside your Father's care. And even the very hairs of your head are all numbered. So don't be afraid; you are worth more than many sparrows." If God cares for the sparrow, then He most certainly cares for us so much. And He cares for our deceased sibling just as much, too.

I pray that as you continue to sift through the details of losing your brother or sister that you will know that your heavenly Father cares about those very details. Know that nothing is outside of God's care for you.

JOURNAL

EXPLORING THE DETAILS

Matthew 10:29-31 says, "Are not two sparrows sold for a penny? Yet not one of them will fall to the ground outside your Father's care. And even the very hairs of your head are all numbered. So don't be afraid; you are worth more than many sparrows."

God is a God of details. He cares for you and all the responsibilities that feel overwhelming. Which duties are you struggling with right now? How can you take it one task at a time? Is there someone whose assistance you can enlist to help you?

What do you need to do, practically speaking, in the aftermath of your sibling's death that will be difficult? How will you go about gathering the courage to do that?

What have you already done that was painful to do?

How can you help other family members do what they need to do? Who can you ask to help you?

CHAPTER FIVE

LETTING OURSELVES GRIEVE

Everyone wanted me to get help and rejoin life, pick up the pieces and move on, and I tried to, I wanted to, but I just had to lie in the mud with my arms wrapped around myself, eyes closed, grieving, until I didn't have to anymore.

Anne Lamott[5]

Grief is like the enemy who launches surprise attacks, hurling sorrow and pain at us at rapid speed, disregarding our pleas for mercy. Just when you think it's safe to come out, the enemy launches another attack.

In those first few days and weeks, the pain is so unbearable. But even as we start to feel it ease up a bit, we find ourselves faced with the intensity of our grief all over again. Something triggers our pain. Maybe it's a standing date we would have had today, except they are gone. Or perhaps we spot a gift they gave us, and we can't restrain the flood of tears. Or perhaps it's the realization, once again, that they are gone and we just miss them. Tears stream down our faces. Our hearts are broken. Grief feels like torrents from a rushing river that threaten to overtake us. Some days, we're drowning in our sorrow.

I have been surprised by grief. Surprised that grief can come upon me so suddenly, when I least expect it. Sometimes even when I am feeling strong...or think I am. Even happy thoughts can suddenly turn sad. Three months after Logan passed away, his younger daughter graduated from college. I was so proud of her accomplishment yet the occasion was tinged with sadness because her dad wasn't at the graduation ceremony. Three years later while thinking about my older niece's new wedding engagement, I felt so happy for her, yet so incredibly sad simultaneously since her daddy wouldn't be at her wedding. I was overcome with tears. An occasion that is supposed to be so happy was tinged with such sadness. These are just two of many bittersweet experiences.

When grief surprises you, sometimes you have to allow it free rein, at least for a little while. Let it wash over you and cleanse you of some of your hurt. When the tears well up in my eyes, there are times when I just have to give myself the grace to grieve. Use that opportunity to cry, pray, journal, or otherwise process your feelings. I've never been much of a "journaler" but lately I have found writing down my thoughts so therapeutic. Not words that anyone else will read, but my own private journal. I can write down my thoughts, or letters to God with all my questions, or even letters to my loved one. The important point is to just write down your thoughts and feelings. Expect it to take time and emotional energy but the end result for me is a sense of peace as I'm able to more fully articulate what would have been just "brain swirls." Journal. Pray. Cry. Do what works for you.

And just when you think it's safe to come outside, expect it to happen again. Grief takes time. Lots of time. Allow it the time it takes. Don't wallow in it, but know you can spend some time grieving and then you can move on. Know that eventually it will be easier, so the surprise attacks by the grief enemy will be fewer and less intense. Healing will happen. It just takes time.

Be patient with yourself. Some experts say those who grieve traverse five stages of loss: denial, anger, bargaining, depression, and acceptance. These stages aren't necessarily meant to be linear. And our grief sometimes doesn't feel very "linear" either. We move back and forth through these various stages. Often we feel like we're taking three steps forward only to take two steps backward. Progress moves at a snail's pace. Don't be discouraged. Your journey through grief may feel very different than these five stages. Just let yourself grieve in your own way and in your own timing. Know it will take time. Lots of time. Keep pressing forward.

I love to read the Psalms. The words from God through folks like David and others are such a comfort to me. Psalm 84 is one of my favorites, especially verses 5-7. "Blessed are those whose strength is in you, whose hearts are set on pilgrimage. As they pass through the Valley of Baka, they make it a place of springs; the autumn rains also cover it with pools. They go from strength to strength, till each appears before God in Zion."

God is indeed our strength. When we set our hearts on walking with him, on finding His presence, we may indeed walk through the Valley of Baka (or Weeping). Yet that place for us becomes refreshing and restorative, like a place of springs. Like an oasis in the desert. I love the image of riding a zipline from pole to pole. We gain momentum and then the next thing we know, we're at the next pole and off we go to ride all over again. With God, we go from strength to strength...like that zipline, until we come face to face with Him in heaven. But all along that zipline of life, we do have His strength to keep us going. We can feel His presence and comfort with us. The good news is we don't have to get to heaven to enjoy these blessings. We can experience God's presence now.

Just like that zipline, God gives us enough strength to make it to the next stop. And again. Day by day. I pray you will claim God's strength for you in His very presence and that you will find refreshment in His spirit and in the comfort of His word. He loves you so very much.

JOURNAL

EXPLORING THE OASIS

Psalm 84:5-7 says, "Blessed are those whose strength is in you, whose hearts are set on pilgrimage. As they pass through the Valley of Baka, they make it a place of springs; the autumn rains also cover it with pools. They go from strength to strength, till each appears before God in Zion."

Is God your strength? If not, ask Him right now to give you strength for each day.

How are you surprised by grief? What thoughts or reminders cause grief to wash over you?

Do you give yourself permission to grieve?

As you walk through the "Valley of Baka" (or Weeping), how can you make it a "Place of Springs", a place of rest and respite? What can you do for yourself today?

CHAPTER SIX

THE YEAR OF "FIRSTS"

They that love beyond the world, cannot be separated by it...
Death is but crossing the world, as friends do the seas;
they live in one another still.

William Penn[6]

It's odd, isn't it, how we remember significant events as to where we were when we heard the news or what date or day of the week it was when something happened. Where were you when the Twin Towers fell? I remember that September 11, 2001, was a Tuesday. Weather-wise, it was a beautiful and sunny day that seemed just too surreal. The quietness of that day in South Carolina was juxtaposed against the chaos and horror in Manhattan. Somehow it didn't seem right for me to have a cloudless day while many miles north, the sky was black with smoke and filled with fire and fumes.

Strange how dates take on new significance when tragedy strikes, how they are indelibly inked into our memories. September 11th is etched into the American memory like no other. You probably have your own dates that you will not forget. For me, my brother passed away on February 17th which was a Tuesday. For many weeks after February 17th, the pain of his absence seemed to be more acute every Tuesday. I marked the passage of time by how many weeks it had been since he was gone. And the 17th of every month suddenly became significant, too. I found that reaching out to family members on those early Tuesdays or 17ths of the month helped me, and I believe also helped them. To everyone else, it was just another Tuesday. Just another 17th. But to us, it was a day and date to remember. In some small way, a day to pay tribute to Logan's life. To allow ourselves the opportunity to grieve a bit so that eventually, the intense pain of those first little anniversaries of his death began to ease a little.

As those anniversaries of your sibling's passing are marked on the calendar in your head, allow yourself the time and space to grieve. It's fine. Actually, it's more than fine. It's totally necessary. Marking the passage of time is healing. Let it be so for you.

But what about the bigger anniversaries? Those "first" anniversaries, like your brother or sister's first birthday after their death. The first Thanksgiving, Christmas, or other significant holiday can be something to dread. Even the first Mother's Day or Father's Day can be difficult. Perhaps the holiday wasn't their own special one. Maybe it's *your* birthday. Regardless, holidays and other family celebrations can be difficult because you know that when you arrive at the appointed destination to get together with family and friends, they won't be there.

The first year of these "firsts" will be difficult. There is no getting around it. Logan died one month before his 49th birthday. On his birthday, we met as a family at his favorite restaurant. It was, as you might expect, bittersweet. It was good to get together with family and friends and share our memories. But it was difficult to see a birthday cake to "Daddy" that his daughters had brought. So very difficult but something they needed to do for their own healing.

Between my brother's birthday and the start of the holiday season, my younger brother and his wife had their first child. Having a new baby at family gatherings helped to distract us, at least on some level. We made it through the first year of "firsts." I think I actually exhaled a sigh of relief to have that first year behind me. Looking forward to the next year didn't seem quite so daunting. I knew since I had survived that first year of anniversaries and holidays that I could survive the next year.

Sometimes we just have to take things one day at a time. Getting through each day may be all we can do. Just putting one foot in front of the other, deliberately and slowly, takes all the energy and effort we can muster. We plod along, day after day, hoping that the passage of time will ease the pain. It does. Eventually. But never as quickly as we'd like.

As I said before, we each grieve in our own way. That is also true for families. Some families when they gather together may totally ignore the fact that one of their members is missing. Others may be able to share memories or at least talk about their loved one. Sometimes one family member may grieve openly while others do not. And sadly, some members may even chastise another for openly grieving. Losing the same person affects each family member differently. When my brother died, I was really worried about my parents. My grandmother, who had outlived three of her four sons as well as her husband, had always said losing a child was such a very difficult loss. My parents and I didn't talk about Logan's passing much. Especially in those early days, it was difficult to know exactly how they were feeling and how they were processing their grief. Being in their early 80's, I think they felt some comfort that they would see Logan in heaven soon. My father did indeed. He passed away two years and ten days after Logan.

Do what you need to do during these "firsts" but reach out to others who are grieving the same loss. Continue the family traditions, even start new ones. Create new memories and relive old ones to keep the memory of your beloved sibling alive while experiencing healing inside yourself.

My prayer for you is that you will be able to move through that first year with the comfort of family and friends as you begin the healing process. I pray that God will give you the strength to begin working through your grief on your own timetable and that you will find yourself stronger at the end of that first year. I pray that you will be able to face the next year with less pain and agony. May it be so.

JOURNAL

EXPLORING COMMEMORATION

What occasions or dates are you expecting to be the most difficult for you?

What can you do to make that day(s) easier?

If you've made it through a special occasion without your sibling, what helped you?   What was especially difficult? Why?

What can you do to commemorate your sibling's passing that would be meaningful to you?

CHAPTER SEVEN

TURNING ASHES INTO BEAUTY

When a parent dies, you lose your past.
When a child dies, you lose your future.

Anonymous

Whoever said that definitely knew loss and grief. A significant part of your past is gone when you lose your parent. And your future is tremendously impacted when you lose a child. Both losses are traumatic. Both are difficult on many levels. But what about when your adult sibling dies? What happens to your past, present, and future?

37

e each share many memories with our siblings. In
__, ʌ huge part of our past is gone when our sibling
dies. My brother Logan had an incredible memory. I teased
him that he could remember events that happened when he
was a baby! How I wish I could remember our past like he
could. Now that he's gone, parts of my past are likewise
gone. No more questions about experiences I can't recall as
clearly. No more laughs with him about our shared
memories. He took that part of my past with him.

Part of my present is gone as well. No more visits
and phone calls and time spent together. No more holidays
together. No more laughs as he would joke about
something, as he often did. No more hugs or smiles or
knowing glances. He took that part of my present with him.

My future is changed forever. No more dreaming
about how we'd spend our retirement years. No shared
moments as our children experience milestones. No more
discussions to plan how in the world we would take care of
our parents as they aged. No advice and opinions about
decisions where he could help. No way to grow older
together. He took that part of my future with him.

So what's left? What's next in this walk with grief?
Know that your future is in God's hands, and He is good.
The Bible tells us in Romans 8:28 that "in all things God
works for the good of those who love him, who have been
called according to his purpose." How can God take
something so painful in our lives and turn it into something
good? What good could possibly come out of our sibling's
death?

God himself is good. He can be trusted to work for
our good. It helps me to think about God and his purpose
for our lives. God's Word to the Israelites in Jeremiah 29:11-
13 says: "For I know the plans I have for you," declares the
Lord, "plans to prosper you and not to harm you, plans to

give you hope and a future. Then you will call on me and come and pray to me, and I will listen to you. You will seek me and find me when you seek me with all your heart." God DOES have a plan for our lives and a new future, even though we may be uncertain as to what that future looks like. Even though we may not want to welcome that new future right now. There may still be tear-stained days from time to time as grief catches us unawares. But know you will survive. It *will* get easier.

What is God's plan for me? How has Logan's death changed me and my future? Just as a wound heals but leaves a scar, so are we changed by our pain in hopefully positive ways, like being more compassionate and more Christ-like. We can use our pain to show comfort and understanding to those God places in our path. We can empathize with others who have lost loved ones, and they know we understand. They are not alone because we've been there, too.

Logan's death has impacted me on many levels and in so many ways. Seeing him die so suddenly and at such a young age, I believe it is important to follow your dreams, to do now what you've been waiting to do later, perhaps in "retirement." Logan was just five months away from retiring. I know he had been looking forward to it. As I've reflected on my own life, there are things I want to do and places I want to see. I'm "working my list" now, as much as I can. Life is too short. So, if there are items on your bucket list, start working them now.

And how precious life really is! Logan's death made me realize not only how short life can be, but also the importance of relationships. I'm thankful for the family and friends that *are* here. Make the most of the time with them, regardless of whether it is through phone calls, visits, emails, or text messages. Keep your accounts with them short.

Ephesians 4:26 says, "Do not let the sun go down while you are still angry." Cherish the moments you have with them. And above all else, tell those you love that you love them. And often. You never know when that opportunity to say "I love you" will be gone forever.

When you call to mind a memory of your beloved brother or sister and you find yourself smiling, you'll know you've crossed over a bridge to the other side of grief where you can think about your sibling in such a way that it isn't as painful as it once was. You're making progress. There will always be a hole in your heart where they were but that hole will become less gaping and more manageable with time. I promise.

In Isaiah 61:2-3, the prophet says God has sent him "to comfort all who mourn, and provide for those who grieve in Zion - to bestow on them a crown of beauty instead of ashes, the oil of joy instead of mourning, and a garment of praise instead of a spirit of despair." God can and will, if we let Him, take the ashes of our grief and transform them into a work of beauty, a beautiful crown for us to wear so that God will be praised. My prayer for you is that you will allow God to work in your heart, to turn your ashes into beauty, to heal you, and to grow you into the person He wants you to be. Never forget God is with you. Jesus tells us in Matthew 28:20 that "surely I am with you always, to the very end of the age." Claim that promise today for your own. And look for opportunities to turn your own ashes into beauty. Amen.

JOURNAL

EXPLORING THE FUTURE

How does losing your sibling impact your past? Your present? Your future?

How has this painful time strengthened you? In what ways have you grown through it?

Name at least one way God is using this pain in your life for good.

"Praise be to the God and Father of our Lord Jesus Christ, the Father of compassion and the God of all comfort, who comforts us in all our troubles, so that we can comfort those in any trouble with the comfort we ourselves receive from God." (2 Corinthians 1:3-4) Is there someone you know who has lost a loved one that you can comfort?

Psalm 90:12 says, "Teach us to number our days, that we may gain a heart of wisdom."

Ephesians 5:15-16 says, "Be very careful, then, how you live – not as unwise but as wise, making the most of every opportunity…"

Life is short. Ponder how short life can be. What will you do differently with your life now?

PHOTOGRAPHY NOTES

All photographs are original by the author during her travels in the United States, Canada, and France.

Cover Photograph: Mountain Bluebells, near Kananaskis, Alberta, Canada.

Introduction: Pathway at Muir Woods, Marin County, California

Chapter One: Road south of Cape Meares, Oregon

Chapter Two: Prickly Pear Cactus, Sedona, Arizona

Chapter Three: Mystery Valley, Arizona

Chapter Four: North shore of Maui, Hawaii

Chapter Five: Wahkeena Falls, Oregon

Chapter Six: Claude Monet's Water Lily Pond, Giverny, France

Chapter Seven: Aspens at Muleshoe, Bow Valley Parkway, Alberta, Canada

ENDNOTES

[1] Bailey, Philip James. *Festus: A Poem.* New York: James Miller, Publishers, 1872. Public domain.

[2] Longfellow, Henry Wadsworth. *Michael Angelo: A Dramatic Poem.* Boston: Houghton, Mifflin and Company, 1884. Public domain.

[3] Smith, Hannah Whitall. *The God of All Comfort.* London: James B. Nisbet & Company, Limited, 1906. Public domain.

[4] Tolstoy, Leo. *Anna Karenina.* Moscow: The Russian Messenger, 1878. Public domain.

[5] Lamott, Anne. *Operating Instructions: A Journal of My Son's First Year.* Copyright © 1993 by Anne Lamott. Used by permission of Pantheon Books, an imprint of the Knopf Doubleday Publishing Group, a division of Random House LLC. All rights reserved. Any third party use of this material, outside of this publication, is prohibited. Interested parties must apply directly to Random House for permission.

[6] Penn, William. *Some Fruits of Solitude.* New York: H.M. Caldwell Company, 1903. Public domain.

Made in the USA
Columbia, SC
27 February 2021